W9-CFB-885

X-Library: Friends of
Lake County Public Library

BRAINJUICE

ENGLISH

fresh squeezed!

For Sam—write on!
—C. D. S.

3 3113 02284 3090

Text copyright © 2004 by Carol Diggory Shields
Illustrations copyright © 2004 by Tony Ross
Jacket design by Todd Sutherland
Interior design by E. Friedman
All rights reserved
CIP Data is available
BrainJuice is a registered trademark of Handprint Books

Published in the United States in 2004 by Handprint Books
413 Sixth Avenue
Brooklyn, New York 11215
www.handprintbooks.com

First Edition
Printed in China
ISBN: 1-59354-053-1
2 4 6 8 10 7 5 3 1

40 thirst-for-knowledge–quenching poems by
CAROL DIGGORY SHIELDS

illustrations by
TONY ROSS

LAKE COUNTY PUBLIC LIBRARY

HANDPRINT BOOKS ✋ BROOKLYN, NEW YORK

Dear Mr. Norman,

When I was in your English classes, back at North Shore School, you probably thought I was two different people. And maybe I was!

First, there was Good Carol, who would happily open her library book for reading or reach for pencil and paper to write poems. And then there was Bad Carol, who turned sullen and mean when it was time to diagram sentences, practice spelling and vocabulary, and ponder punctuation.

For years Good Carol and Bad Carol had their own private war, even while the two of us (somehow!) became a librarian and had some poems published. Looking back, I realize now that Good Carol just wanted to read and write for the fun of it, without having to learn all that boring stuff about commas and semicolons and verb tenses and prepositions.

But over the years, something you had been trying to get across to us about English kept nagging at me. So much so, that I had to do something about it.

You'll be happy to know that I made a list of all those frustrating English rules and tools from school, compressed it into basic facts, and then condensed it even further into forty poems. And, behold! Brainjuice! Probably even Bad Carol wouldn't have minded learning these facts, as long as they were disguised as poetry.

Whether you were dealing with me when I was happily immersed in *The Lord of the Rings* or when I was kicking the furniture over agreement of subject and verb, you were always patient, kind, and inspiring. Maybe you will try a little BrainJuice in your English classes. Just imagine— a whole class of Good Carols! Well, let's not get carried away.

With fondest of memories,

Your former student,
Carol Diggory Shields

THE RULES

The rules of English must be obeyed,
Don't panic or even feel dismayed.
There are hints and tips to help you cope.
Grammar's confusing—hang on,
There's hope!

There are 10,782 rules for perfect grammar, here reduced to a mere 14, including:

- "I before e, except after c," unless the word is *eight*, *Keith*, *protein*, *neighbor*, *weird*, or one of fifty other exceptions.

- How to make adverbs swiftly, brilliantly, painlessly.

- What happens when a noun and a verb fall in love?

"English usage is sometimes more than mere taste, judgment, and education—
sometimes it's sheer luck, like getting across the street."
—E. B. White (1899–1985)

Surrounded

Nouns, nouns, they're everywhere,

The earth, the sun, the water, the air.

Some nouns are concrete, for example, a brick.

It's real, it's heavy (ouch!), and it's thick.

While abstract nouns are hard to define,

Some of them only exist in our minds,

Like hope and peace, love and freedom—

We know they're real, but it's hard to see them.

Common nouns are just any old words:

Bubblegum, backpacks, shoelaces, birds.

While proper nouns are quite specific

(Your name is proper—don't you feel terrific?),

Maria and Annie, Jed and Camilla,

As well as Wisconsin, New York, and Godzilla.

Possessive and plural nouns, singular too,

We're surrounded by nouns, whatever we do!

"All nouns are abbreviations . . . instead of saying 'receding sun' and 'oncoming darkness', we say 'twilight.'" —Jorge Luis Borges (1899–1986)

Verbless

If you didn't have verbs, you'd be in a muddle.

You couldn't get up if you fell in a puddle.

You'd be in a pickle, a jam, and a mess,

Couldn't get out of bed or even get dressed.

Without any verbs, you'd be plum out of luck,

No walking, no talking—you'd really be stuck.

Verbs are a lot like the wheels on a car,

Without any wheels—well, it wouldn't go far.

So if conjugation should give you a pain,

You'll notice you even need verbs to complain.

"Considering that we use it so often, it is really too bad that the verb 'to be' has to be the most irregular, slippery verb in the language."
—*The Guide to Grammar and Writing*

To Be or Not to Be

The prize for irregularity
Has got to go to the small verb "be."
"I be, he bees," should be the norm,
But "I am, he is" is the present form.
The past tense usually adds "e-d,"
But that would be just too e-z,
Instead the past is "were" and "was."
Why is this? Just because.
No wonder "to be" and its conjugations
Confuses those from many nations.

Who Are We?

You and *I* are not alike,
But *we* are both the same.
They are not like *us*, and yet they are.
(Can you guess our name?)

This and *that* are similar,
But different as can be,
And though those two don't know it,
She is the same as *he*.

Some resemble others,
It's crazy but it's true,
And *his* and *hers* are just like *ours*.
(Need another clue?)

We're possessive, interrogative,
Demonstrative, reflective.
If you figured out we're pronouns,
Then you're a good detective.

They're Everywhere!

First *ahead*! Then far *behind*!
They just refuse to be confined.
They're *near* and *far*, *there* and *here*,
Like monkeys *on* a chandelier.
Over, *under*, *across*, and *through*,
Inside, *outside*, *between* the two,
Within, *without*, *among*, *around*,
It's hard to pin a preposition *down*.

Living and Breathing

Adjectives can be *short* and *fat*,
Warm and *cuddly* as Grandma's cat,
Or *long* and *lanky*, *skinny* and *lean*,
Tough and *dry* as an *old* string bean.
Goofy, *giggly*, *kooky*, *silly*,
Creepy, *scary*, *dark*, and *chilly*,

"For me, a page of good prose is where one hears the rain [and] the noise of battle." —John Cheever (1912–1982)

Like a *simple* sketch in black,

Nouns can outline *basic* facts,

But to make a picture that really lives,

Give it *some* color with adjectives!

Adverbcadabra

A handy little secret
To you I'll gladly give—
Watch me make an adverb
From an adjective.

Please hand me an adjective—
Ah, "magical"—quite nice.
I'll stick an "l-y" on the end,
Wave my black wand twice.
Now close your eyes and let's all count,
One . . . two . . . three.
Open them and you'll behold
The adverb "magically"!

Status of My Homework Assignment about Contractions

Could've.
Would've.
Didn't.
Should've.

Rools

Spelling rools, spelling rools,

I think that they were made by fules.

I study them until I druel.

(And drueling is not very cewl.)

I study them at home and skool,

I think these ruels are very crool.

The British edition of *English Grammar for Beginners* (Macmillan, 1928) by Llewelyn Tipping lists forty possible verb tenses.

Tension

Past, present, and future—they are all fine.

But more tenses than those? Let's draw the line!

The "present perfect" gives me a cow

(Means started before and continuing now).

While something that started and later was finished,

Like, "I had been hungry, till I ate my spinach,"

Calls for the use of the "past perfect" tense.

Then there's "future perfect" (is this making sense?),

Which means that an action hasn't begun,
But will in the future, and then will be done.
For example, "I'm hoping that I will have read
The rest of my book before I go to bed."
And please, let's not mention the perfect progressive,
Because if you do I'll turn deeply depressive.
All of these choices! Can't we condense?
Too many tenses are making me tense!

Sentence Romance

A verb and noun met up one day.

Said the verb, "I think you're sweet!

Together, you and I could form a sentence that's complete."

Noun winked. Verb grinned. A simple life they lived.

She gave him several adverbs, he brought her an adjective.

They added a conjunction, and when the time was ripe,

They had a little clause, of the independent type.

Prepositions followed, and then, without a pause,

They found they were the parents

Of a cute dependent clause.

The noun and verb both smiled and sighed,

"Our sentence sure has grown.

Though it is now compound-complex,

It's still our home sweet home."

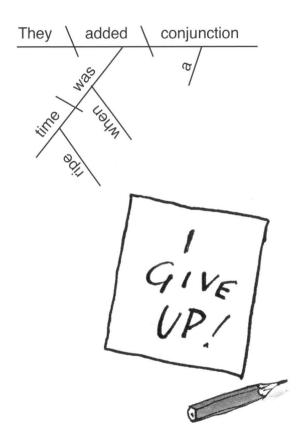

"Ask me no questions, and I'll tell you no fibs."
—Oliver Goldsmith (1730?–1774)

Why?

I wonder why, I wonder why
I'm such an interrogative guy?
I ask, "Who, what, where, and when?"
You answer. Guess what? I ask again.
I'm quizzical, questioning, bumped, and slumped,
But most of all, I'm always stumped.
Perpetually puzzled and in the dark,
Such is the life of a question mark.

"An exclamation point is used to mark an outcry or an emphatic or ironical comment. In order not to detract from its effectiveness, however, the author should use it sparingly."
—*The Chicago Manual of Style*, fifteenth edition

Do you suffer from dull and listless writing?
Use exclamation marks! They're so exciting!
Use one! Or two!! Or even three!!!
They seem to holler, "Hey, look at me!"
Keep your readers from dozing and snoring,
Exclamation marks! They're never boring!
Yippee! Hooray! What's that you say?

You want me to shut up and go away!

Punctuation Promenade

The punctuation marks went walking,
On a day that was sunny and bright,
They started out at half-past noon,
And didn't get home till night.
The comma kept pausing briefly,
For just a little rest,
The parentheses said, "Hurry up!
(That comma is such a pest.)"

The dash was like the comma—
Taking short breaks—too.
The colon was introducing lists,
"Here's what we need to do:"
Semi-colon was joining up
Some phrases that seemed related,
"We're not getting anywhere;
This walk's too complicated."

Ellipsis skipped from word to word,
Leaving some parts out,
"Hey . . . let's . . . stop . . . go . . ."
He would yell and shout.
Hyphen put things together,
Helter-skelter, willy-nilly,
While underlining emphasized,
"You are <u>all</u> just acting <u>silly</u>!"
Apostrophe kept contracting,
"Let's run, let's jump, let's hop."
At the end of every sentence,
Period, of course, had to stop.
The quotation marks talked on and on,
"Yakkity, yakkity, yak."
It really is a wonder
That they ever made it back.

THE TOOLS

Are you all uptight about writing right?
We've got the tools to solve your plight.
Use alliteration, use interjection
For writing that is near perfection!

Included are handy tools to make order out of chaos, such as:

- Meet the Nyms: Synonyms, antonyms, and homonyms.

- Oh ho! Palindromes!

- Is a simile like a metaphor?

Cuneiform (kyu ni E form): Looking something like bird footprints, cuneiform started out as simple pictures made by reeds pressed into clay. Like hieroglyphics, the pictures were combined to make words and sentences.

The ABC's of the ABC's

In ancient Sumeria, back in the day,

People made marks with sticks on clay,

Counting wheat and cattle herds,

Using pictures in place of words.

The nearby Phoenicians said, "This cuneiform's swell!

But marks could stand for sounds as well,

Each mark we make could be a letter,

And letters make words—that's even better!"

The Phoenicians sailed off, across the seas,
Taking along their ABC's.
They sailed to Greece, and the Greeks they met
Also needed an alphabet.
Greeks borrowed the letters, added some new.
The Romans came next and changed a few,
Which remain the same, in most every way,
As the alphabet we still use today!

"England and America are two countries separated by the same language."
—George Bernard Shaw (1856–1950)

English or English

Do you speak English or do you speak English?
There is a difference, I fear,
The English they speak in England
Is different from that spoken here.
In the rain over here, you'd use an umbrella,
Over there, they use a brolly.
Boots are Wellies, and a shopping cart,
In England, is called a trolley.

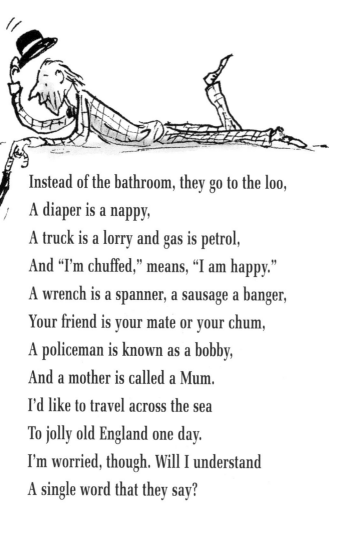

Instead of the bathroom, they go to the loo,
A diaper is a nappy,
A truck is a lorry and gas is petrol,
And "I'm chuffed," means, "I am happy."
A wrench is a spanner, a sausage a banger,
Your friend is your mate or your chum,
A policeman is known as a bobby,
And a mother is called a Mum.
I'd like to travel across the sea
To jolly old England one day.
I'm worried, though. Will I understand
A single word that they say?

Interjection Connection

Yo! Come on down and check our selections
Of totally fabulous interjections.
You'll shout "Hurray!" and "Whoop-dee-do"
When you find the perfect one for you.
We've got "Oops" and "Egad" and also "Yikes"
For those who are the klutzy types.

"Speak properly, and in as few words as you can, but always plainly;
for the end of speech is not ostentation, but to be understood."
—William Penn (1644-1718)

"Eek!" "Good gracious," and "Oh my, my!"
Are for the soft spoken and kind of shy.
As well as "Yay, defense!" and assorted screams
To cheer on your favorite sporting teams.
You'll find perfection in every section—
At your local Interjection Connection!

Meet the Palindromes

Come over and meet the Palindrome clan,
"This is Mom, Dad, Otto, Bob, and Nan."
Their favorite things are like each one's name—
Backward or forward, spelled the same.
Their dog is named Pup and Lil is the cat,
Dad likes to kayak, and Mom likes to tat.
Nan drives a Civic, and Bob a racecar,

A palindrome reads the same backward or forward:
Eva, can I stab bats in a cave?

Otto says, "A Toyota—the best by far."

Their car horns don't beep, they go "Toot-toot,"

When the weather is warm, Dad says, "Too hot to hoot!"

They get up at noon, in the eve stay up late,

"STEP ON NO PETS" says the sign on their gate.

"No lemons, no melon," is the old family motto,

Of Bob and Nan, Mom, Dad, and Otto.

Awesomely Alliterated

It's awesome, astounding, and animated,

Adorable and appreciated,

Amazing, amusing, alphabetically active,

Appealing, artistic, and attractive.

Applaud aloud in admiration,

Always alluring—alliteration.

Onomatopoeia (ON-uh-mat-uh-PEE-uh): words that imitate the sounds they represent. Different languages may have different sounds —cats say "Meow" in English and in Japanese they say, "Nya-nya."

Clickety-Clack

Clickety-clack, clickety-clack, click-click-clack,
Hear that train goin' down the track,
When the engine rumbles with that big bass sound,
You know you're onomatopoeia bound.

The whistle shrieks and the bells ding-dong,
The locomotive chugs a choo-choo song,
The wind swooshes by and the silver rails whine,
Ridin' on that onomatopoeia line.

Whoo-whoo!

Searching

My brain is busy as a bee,

Searching for a simile,

Thoughts are twirling like a top.

Fizzing round like soda pop,

I'm determined as an old bloodhound,

Or Sherlock Holmes—I'll track one down.

I know that similes exist,
They can't just vanish like the mist!
Thick as a brick, I feel so dumb,
My mind aches like a hammered thumb.
Like a march through mud—it's too hard for me.
I'll never find a simile.

Metaphorically Speaking

There's an empty space inside of me,
A cavern dark and deep,
From down inside come echoing roars—
A dragon awaking from deep sleep.
The dragon rumbles louder,
The thunder of a storm at night,
When we hide our heads under pillows
And cover our eyes in fright.
I pray for an aproned, hair-netted angel
With the magical key to the gate,
Who'll fly down to my rescue
And save me from this fate.

So maybe I'm overdoing it,
With all these metaphors,
But it's 12:14 and I'm starving—
Please open the lunchroom doors!

"A synonym is a word you use when you can't spell the word you first thought of." —Burt Bacharach

Speaking Greek

Here's a little Greek for you,
"Nym" is the word for *name*,
"Ant" is Greek for *opposite*,
While "syn" means it's the *same*.
For words that are a lot alike,
Like *skinny*, *lean*, and *slim*,
Use the "sym" paired with the "nym,"
And you've got a *synonym*.
For opposites like *fat* and *thin*,
High and *low*, or *bright* and *dim*,
Put "ant" and "nym" together,
Ta-da! An *antonym*!

36 Ways to Say Cool

It's groovy, great, the cat's meow,

It's awesome, chill, it's phat, it's wow.

Neat and smashing, fab and slick,

Tuff and super, dope and sick.

It's marvy, dandy, swell, divine,

Nifty, peachy-keen, so fine.

Hunky-dory, righteous, rad,

The bomb, far-out, it's good, it's bad.

It rules, it rocks, it's fly, it's tight,

It's nice, okay, and well, all right.

How Many Homonyms?

When he ate eight pairs of pears.
My dear deer grew quite sickly,
But the doc by the dock, his herd had heard,
Could cure him pretty quickly.

They said, "He helped our aunt's pet ant
And cured a hairless hare.
He fixed a horse who was quite hoarse
And saved a poor bare bear."

We traveled in a daze for days
Till at last we peered at the pier.
Though my dear deer had been weak all week,
We knew that help was near.

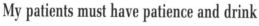

The doctor said, "Son, rest here in the sun
And see the sea for a while.
My patients must have patience and drink
A vial of this medicine vile."

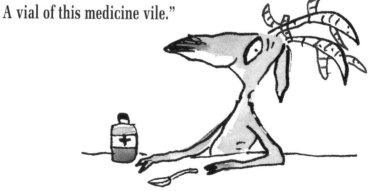

"He'll heal very soon," the doctor said,

We were sure by the shore this was true.

And when the deer called, "Hey, give me some hay!"

He was good as new, we knew.

SCHOOL (AND BEYOND)

Both in school and later, if you want to succeed,
Reading and writing are what you will need.
We'll teach you techniques of communication,
That will help you a lot, even post-graduation.

Let's face it, even after graduation you'll be reading
and writing. In this section, you will find life-time skills for:

- Writing an RL (Real Letter) instead of an IM.

- Standing up in front of a group without falling
  on your face.

- Acquiring a huge, impressive, awe-inspiring,
  splendid, effective vocabulary with just the
  turn of a page.

"All good books are alike in that they are truer than if they had really happened and after you are finished reading one you will feel that all that happened to you and afterwards it belongs to you . . ." —Ernest Hemingway (1899–1961)

I Need a Book!

I need a book for a book report,
Something good and something short.
A hero, a villain, a plot that's strong,
Plenty of action (but not too long).

A book that is thrilling, beyond belief,
Suspenseful, well written, and also brief.
Something with depth, with humor and power,
A book I can read in the next half-hour.

"In a survey of 3,000 people, most of them feared public speaking more than they feared death."
—Cristina Stuart, *How to Be an Effective Speaker*

Oral Report

I have to give my oral report
Tomorrow morning in school.
Some people might be nervous,
But I am calm and cool.
Did research at the library
And on the Internet.
Copied down what I found out,
So I would not forget.
Wrote an outline and rough draft,
Checked pronunciation,
Polished up the final version
Of my presentation.
My index cards are organized,
Lined up nice and straight.
And I'm hoping that the world will end

Tomorrow, just after 8.

The Outline

I. Outlines can really help you out,

    A. When your thoughts

        1.   Are muddled and
        2.   Scattered about.

    B. When it's time to write,

        1.   But you don't have a clue and
        2.   Your research makes no sense to you,

II. Start writing those numerals,

A. Roman-style.

B. You'll discover

   1.   That in a while,
   2.   Those mixed-up notes
   3.   (That you've been dreading)
   4.   Each will have its own subheading.

III. At the final entry, called conclusion,

A. You will feel much less confusion.

B. And you will find, to your surprise,

C. Your paper just got organized!

"Dancing in all its forms cannot be excluded from the curriculum . . . ;
dancing with the feet, with ideas, with words . . . and with the pen."
—Friedrich Nietzsche (1844–1900)

Poetry Dances

Poetry dances along on feet,
A foot is where you find the beat.
If the beat goes da-DUM, da-DUM, da-DUM,
That's called iambic, it's like a drum.
Now give a small skip, and turn it around,
To a DUM-da, DUM-da, DUM-da sound.

"Do not commit your poems to pages alone. Sing them, I pray you."
—Virgil (70 B.C.–19 B.C.)

Keep it up and don't be pokey,
A beat like this is called a trochee.
Pick up the pace, to more of a trot,
DUM-da-da, DUM-da-da, ready or not."
That is dactylic, but don't stop to rest,
We're galloping onward toward anapest—
Da-da-DUM, da-da-DUM, da-da-DUM.
Now go on out there and dance up a poem!

Poetry Assignment #1: Haiku

Must write haiku poem.
Do not know how to do it.
There. Now it is done.

"One ought, every day at least, to hear a little song, read a good poem,
see a fine picture . . ."
—Johann Wolfgang von Goethe (1749–1832)

Poetry Assignment #2: Limerick

A kid in an English class

Once wrote a limerick real fast,

So fast that, no joking,

The paper was smoking,

And his pencil blew up with a blast.

Poetry Assignment #3: Blank Verse

I love blank verse,

Because

It does not

Have to

Rhyme.

And,

At long, long last,

I can write

A poem

About

An

Orange.

Poetry Assignment #4: Shape Poem

When you write a poem
it
just
might fly,
like a kite soaring
up in the sky. Sailing far
away from you. Still
someone may see
it up in the blue
and say,
Hey,
I have felt that way too.

Poetry Assignment #5: The Epic

An epic poem should be grand and big,
Something to flip your teacher's wig.
This will do without a doubt—
I'll write how English came about!

This English language? What a crazy brew!
A mixed-up, ever-changing stew.
Did the first English settlers growl and grunt?
Say "Murf org mooga—Go mammoth hunt?"
We really don't know just what they said.
They built Stonehenge, and now they're dead.
Next came the Celts, whose words are found
In names like York and London-town,
And rivers flowing to the sea,
The Avon, Thames, and the Rye, and Dee.

"The universe is made of stories, not of atoms."
—Muriel Ruykeyser (1913–1980)

The Romans came and stayed awhile,
Brought Latin to the English isle,
Words like *candle*, *wine*, and *cheese*,
Cats and *onions*, *kettle* and *peas*.
They built roads and indoor plumbing,
But scurried home when Goths were coming,
No sooner had they waved, "*Vale!*"
When the Anglo-Saxons came to stay,

Joining other tribes Germanic,
To push Celts seaward in a panic.
These tribes brought words like *house* and *meat*,
Child, man, wife, live, fight, and *eat.*
They loved to tell heroic stories
(Some like *Beowulf*, quite gory),
But couldn't read or write things down
Until the Christians came around,

Bringing pen and pencil sets
As well as handy alphabets.
Books were written, life was good,
Till Vikings sailed into the 'hood.
The Norsemen came to dominate,
But brave King Alfred set them straight,
Kept Vikings to the Northern region
That's why we speak English—not Norwegian,
Though they added words like *dazzle* and *rake*,
Sister, *freckle*, *dirt*, *root*, *take*.
Things settled down, and then came stormin",
William and his gang of Normans.
They overran the English isle—
Soon speaking French was all the style—
Words like *money*, *pastry*, *flower*,
Sausage, *prison*, *prince*, and *power*.

With the crowning of Queen Bess,
And Mr. Caxton's printing press,
The English language hit high gear.
Plays by good old Will Shakespeare
Widened folks' vocabulary,
As did Johnson's dictionary.
The stew was a-bubble, soon to expand,
Spreading out to distant lands.
Taking new flavors, bold and saucy,
Cajun, Spanglish, Krio, Aussie.
African American, Creole, Canadian,
Jamaican, Kiwi, Trinidadian.
Each alike and yet unique,
This awesome language that we speak.

The Word

It's the perfect word for my essay.
It wraps things up quite neatly,
And if it means what I think it means,
It expresses my thoughts completely.

I'll get an "A" for sure,
And note—"Extraordinary!"
My classmates all will be impressed
With my great vocabulary.

I know just how it sounds,
I can whisper it and yell it.
I really need to look it up,
But I don't know how to spell it.

"When you have a word in mind, but you need to find out the meaning, you use a dictionary . . .

What's Another Word for Thesaurus?

I think the thesaurus is really cool,
An extremely helpful reference tool.
Like, if your brother is driving you crazy,
Don't call him a brat—that's just lazy.
Use the thesaurus, dive right in,
You'll find far better synonyms,
Like *nitwit, twerp, squirt,* or *tadpole,*
Guttersnipe, dolt, rascal, or *troll,*
Grommet, goofball, pill, halfwit,
Whippersnapper, pest, punk, or *twit.*
If Mom gets mad and makes you explain,
You can say that you were using your brain
(Your *think-tank,* your *noggin, gray matter,* or *bean*)
And being quite *quick-witted, sharp, shrewd,* and *keen.*

The Letter

The Heading: the place for your address
The date should also go here,
This section's called The Salutation,
(A fancy way to say "Dear").
This part of the letter is called The Body,
Where you say why you're writing the letter,
For example: "Thank you, Grandma dear,
For the green, orange, purple-pink sweater."
The Closing part, where you should put
"Yours truly," or "Sincerely,"
Signature means sign your name
(Be sure and write it clearly).
P.S. Stands for Post Script, where you can add
The things that you almost forgot.
Such as, P.S. Grandma, I love you,
And I really miss you a lot!

The Heading
(your address)
The date

The Salutation:

The Body,
(Where you say what why you're writing
the letter)

The Closing,
Signature

P.S. (Post Script)

"It is not a bad idea to get in the habit of writing down one's thoughts.
It saves one having to bother anyone else with them."
—Isabel Colegate

Dear Journal,

It's journal-writing time,
And I don't know what to do.
My life is very boring,
Nothing interesting or new.
But the teacher's looking at me,
So I guess I'd better try,
I think I'll tell you, journal,
About what's going on nearby.

Ann and Chris are passing notes,
Jon's whispering to Ted,
Sammy's aiming spitballs
At the back of Nathan's head.
Amy's drawing horses,
Jed's designing rocket ships,
Dan is building bridges
Out of silver paper clips.
Roy is sneaking bites of lunch,
Chad is racing ants,
Julio is poking holes
In the knees of his new pants.
Sara's writing madly
(She's on journal number four).

Tad looks like he is thinking,
But he just began to snore.
Our teacher says "Time's up,
Journal writing's done."
I can't believe it's over—
This writing stuff is fun!

Title Index by Section

The Rules

The Tools

School (and Beyond)

Title Index

LAKE COUNTY PUBLIC LIBRARY

3 3113 02284 3090

JUV 811.54 SHIE
Shields, Carol Diggory.
English, fresh squeezed

LAKE COUNTY PUBLIC LIBRARY
INDIANA

AD	FF	MU
AV	GR	NC
BO	HI	SJ
CL	HO	CNL 7-05
DS	LS	

Some materials may be renewable by phone or in person if there are
no reserves or fines due.   www.lakeco.lib.in.us   LCP#0390